Caught in Time

The Songs and Poetry of Jane Eamon

Jane Eamon

Manor House

Caught in Time

Library and Archives Canada Cataloguing in Publication

Eamon, Jane
    Caught in time : the songs and poems of Jane Eamon / Jane Eamon.

ISBN 978-1-897453-19-3

    I. Title.

PS8609.A56C38 2011   C811'.6
C2011-907692-6

Copyright 2011-08-30 by Jane Eamon
Published November 28, 2011
Manor House Publishing Inc.
(905) 648-2193 www.manor-house.biz

First Edition. 96 pages. All rights reserved.
Cover design: Michael Davie/Donovan Davie

Cover photo: Jane Eamon
Contact Info: janeeamon@shaw.ca

Printed in Canada.

We acknowledge the financial support of the Government of Canada through the Canada Book Fund for our publishing activities.

A BIT OF GRACE
(Recorded on Caught In Time, 2010)

I can say without regrets
that I've done the best I could
Though sometimes I forget
it wasn't always good
But I won't beat myself up thinking
of the maybe and the should
If truth be told, I've lived my life
like I hoped I would

The lovers I have known
are here in my mind's eye
Everyone of them a home
Though I can't remember why
Was it something in that moment
caught me as I happened by
I'm wedded to them now
like a bridegroom to a bride

I will shout it from the rooftops
Hear me roar for I am here
Sing it to the masses
as I whisper in their ear
Tales and broken sonnets
just enough to keep them near
I admit it's the silence that I fear

I'll keep on keeping on
A little slower every day
Do everything I can
to mold this lump of clay
If that bronze is slow to casting
It'll break apart someday
and when it does I hope I find
a little bit of grace

PIECE OF RED CLAY
(Recorded on Caught In Time, 2010)

I walked today in the red dirt
Saw the land at its raw birth
And wondered at my worth in this world
I put my hands on the old stone
Heard the whispering of old souls
Still living and breathing in this earth

Everything that I'd been thinking
Seemed to disappear
Somehow spirit
Brought me here

These stones have been shaped
With a patient hand and grace
Every tower changing face over years
And in my quest for an answer
I missed what they stand for
but I found myself moved to tears

And the staggering thought
Of what they must have seen
It's hard to explain

I took photos that day
Hoping maybe in that way
I'll get what they're
Trying to say to me
And I was blessed by the beauty
And I'll carry it with me
In this tiny little piece of red clay

SALVATION FOR THE STREET
(Recorded on Caught In Time, 2010)

Sunday morning in the mission
the junkies are asleep
There's a tiny storefront chapel
That you can barely see
Sister Monica's the sign says
In letters small and neat
Promising salvation for the street

Ain't no church with fancy steeple
Just a crudely painted sign
Dusted up with glitter
Saying dance with the divine
And the Lord he will deliver
Come one, come all inside
Promising salvation for the street

To every hard line pusher
Every bum down on his luck
Every ragged old streetwalker
Who's floundering in the muck
It's the one place all's forgiven
No one's trying to make a buck
Promising salvation for the street

The market on the corner
Is all boarded up and spent
The apartments overhead
Now only hookers tend to rent
But Sister Monica's got the gospel
In a hardened retail tent
Promising salvation for the street

They came to this country
With promise in their eyes
But circumstance and living
Has taught them to survive
They come here every Sunday
Hoping God is still alive
Promising salvation for the street

UNDER THE BIG SKY
(Recorded on Caught In Time, 2010)

It takes a brave man to live on these plains
John Wayne would have loved this
Endless riding the range
Where mountain men prospectors
Still work their claims
Under the big sky

Wild horses still run here I guess
Like the ones who rode
For the pony express
But now they're a tour stop
There to impress
Under the big sky

Under the big sky
Can't help but feel small
And wonder how we got here at all
When the first things you buy
Are a horse and a plough
And hope you make it somehow

It tests the mettle of a man
How much he can bear
When the snow starts a'drifting
And there's nothing out here
But red rock canyons
And pronghorn deer
Under the big sky

There's a rusted old truck
By the side of the road
A marker of sorts
Of the land's heavy load
And the toll that it takes
When you're looking for gold
Under the big sky

GRAVEYARD
(unreleased)

Graveyard is empty
In the bright light of morn
There's flowers on the old stone
Like someone's come callin'
Ribbons line the pathway
There's a fresh grave in the clay
And the wind is soughing
Through the trees

The cross is slowly reeling
From the weight of suicide
The face is cracked and peeling
With its hint of earthly pride
The mourners cry for nothing
The king will not be coming
And the wind is soughing
Through the trees

And all the people come
To sing in unison
And all the monuments
Repeat the sad lament

BEAUTY IN THE RUBBLE
(unreleased)

I'm standing in the middle
Of the rubble
It surrounds me
It's fallen from the life I'd built
And lays scattered in bits
all around me

It was a house of cards, credit cards
With no way, no way out
It left me here with nothing
But empty pockets
And self doubt

But there's beauty in the rubble
It's true
There's beauty in the rubble
Depends on the view

I blamed myself, judged myself
So much it became a label
Lost every hand I'd dealt
And left with cards on the table
I'm gonna pick up a hammer and a chisel
Start slowly chipping away
Find the little piece of sanity, that gem
When I clear this mess away

They say you gotta hit rock bottom
So you can, you can start again
I guess I'll learn the hard way
Or figure out the game
There's no point in getting so hung up
And thinking there's nothing I can do
I'll just pick up that hammer and chisel
And change my point of view

SINGING HALLELUJA
(Recorded on Deep Water 2006)

So desperate to remember
What he came here for
So eager, so breathless
He forgets
The crutches he's been carrying
Lay broken on the floor
And he falls into a sea of old regrets

Ghosts of bridges burning
And the enemies he's made
Leave behind an acrid bitter taste
He's waiting for redemption
Or some way to be saved
And he curses every line on his face
Singing hallelujah

He takes a good long look
At the person in the mirror
Wonders who it is and
Where'd he go
There's no justice to this aging
No reason to his life
Just a silent litany of growing old

Every time he's staggered
'neath the weight of something lost
Now penetrates the fortress he has made
He damns the silent pictures
And thinks about the cost
And hates that it's all stirring up again

He pours another whiskey
Though he's had too much to drink
The ice in the glass the only sound
He lets the voices clamor
To lead him to the brink
As the glass falls empty to the ground

WAITING FOR THE WIND TO CHANGE
(unreleased)

I'm waiting for the wind to change
Hoping somehow
Things will rearrange
There's no comfort in the eye of this storm
When the waves keep crashing
Round my door
I'm running a race I can't win
So tired and feeling all in
So I'm waiting for the wind to change
So I can start again

I've anchored and I've tied up my heart
Hoping somehow
It wouldn't come apart
But the ropes ain't holding it down
It's come undone
And I'm blowing around
I'm hanging on for dear life
Keeping level
Just to make it through the night
So I'm waiting for the wind to change
So I can start again

I hope there's a calm up ahead
Cause it's still blowing and
Raining on my head
And I pray for a light in the dark
At the end of this tunnel
A tiny little spark
What would happen if I just let go
Let the wind come and take me
Anywhere it wants to go
So I'll keep waiting for the wind to change
So I can start again

LONG WAY DOWN
(Recorded on Deep Water 2006)

It's a fine line we're walking on
Hard to tell right from wrong
And if we stumble we're gonna fall
A long way down

One side the devil calls his own
Gonna tempt you to his fiery home
And if you listen you could be gone
A long way down

Lordie, lordie it's so hard to pick and choose
Things get twisted and you don't know what to do
When the good Lord comes a'calling
Saying try to keep it true
That ole devil's gonna sing you the blues

The other side got the angel sweet
Got religion up his sleeve
It might be your ticket, the sure reprieve
To keep you from
The long way down

LOVE IS
(unreleased)

Love doesn't come with instructions
No manual, book you can read
But you close your eyes
And jump off the ledge
To follow where ever it leads

Love doesn't come when you ask it
It sings with its own sense of rhyme
When out of the blue, it happens to you
You sing along every time

I've always thought to have loved and have lost
Is the hardest thing to go through
But if losing is pain, love fills you again and again
It's true

Love doesn't have an agenda
That isn't how it will work
With that first kiss, you'll savour the risk
And bless it for all that its worth

BREAKING DOWN
(unreleased)

Feeling kind of numb
There's static in the air
Waiting for release
Still I am glued to this chair

Trying so hard not to think
I can't figure out what is real
Standing on the brink
Where everything's so surreal

Breaking down, breaking down
Can't seem to find my way through
Breaking down, breaking down
When all I can think of is you

Finding it hard to breathe
When will I start to heal
How can I get relief
This is not the way I should feel....

Breaking down

GOOD EARTH
(Recorded on Deep Water 2006)

There's a wisdom in the river
There's a blessing on the wind
When I feel it, the good earth under my feet
Well I know I'm safely gathered in

Trouble always seems to follow
Every where I try to go
But when I feel it, the good earth
Under my feet
It's the only thing I need to know

There's a wisdom

There are bibles, there are preachers
There are those who search in vain
For an answer, or just some comfort, Lord
To ease their waking pain

There's a wisdom

I stand with my feet planted here
Lift my eyes towards the sky
When I feel it, the good earth under my feet
It's a strength I know I cannot buy

There's a wisdom

LAY ME DOWN
(Recorded on Deep Water 2006)

Lay me down in the clover
Let the wind wash my face
Will you weep when it's over
And I leave this place
Whisper to the grasses
Saying here is my grave
Lay me down in the clover
Let the wind wash my face

Lay me down by the river
Let the rocks cover me
Will you still be a'callin
Wondering where I might be
I'm a long way from you, dear
Returned to the sea
Lay me down by the river
Let the rocks cover me

Lay me down in the forest
Let the trees take to root
Will you let the green ivy
Wind its way round my boot
I hear a bird, she's calling
And looking to roost
Lay me down in the forest
Let the trees take to root

Lay me down in your heart dear
Let nothing replace
When I'm back to the earth
Will you still hold a trace
Of the woman I once was
And a bittersweet taste
Lay me down in your heart dear
Let nothing replace

DEEP WATER
(Recorded on Deep Water 2006)

Deep water, muddy water, old memory
Gotta cross it, get across it
Won't let me be
Lord I'm weary but I will stand
Freedom's calling from the promised land
Deep water, muddy water, old memory

Deep water, muddy water, old memory
Gotta cross it, get across it
Won't let me be
I hear you Lord, what you telling me to do
But the water's so deep
And I can't see into that
Deep water, muddy water, old memory

Deep water, muddy water, old memory
Gotta cross it, get across it
Won't let me be
I'm wading in Lord, hold to my hand
Current come and take me
So I can stand in this
Deep water, muddy water, old memory

ONE LAST SONG
(Recorded on Deep Water 2006)

Tonight we gathered in this place
For the music
For stories of travels and things
I shared a secret, made you laugh
And wonder at the beauty
In these silver strings
Maybe we cried, but I know that it's okay
The music inside this old guitar
Has to be played
And every bright chord and the words
That I sang
Echoed here tonight

And I'll sing one last song before I go
A simple melody
One we all should know
And if you care to, come sing it with me now
This one last song before I go

It's funny how the music
Can tug at the heart strings
Make memories painfully clear
It shows us that we're human
And frailty's so precious
It's something most infinitely dear
I sing with the wisdom of the old soul
Inside me
Play with the hands of a child
And I'll share my religion
Each time that we gather if only for a little while

And I'll sing one last song

THE SOLDIER'S LAMENT
(Recorded on Real 2008)

Lord I've been thinking here in the mud
That maybe you've gone away
I'm tired, stinking and smelling of blood
And I don't have the strength to pray

For too many days now I've lived in this hole
No water, no food, no rest
The rain it keeps coming and everything's dark
And I hope that this day ain't my last

I saw Jimmy fall, took a bullet to the head
He died in the dirt where he lay
I took his boots, I needed them bad
He'd no use for them anyway

Lord, can I ask you why am I here
In this hell that I don't deserve
Salvation ain't coming on the end of this gun
It's more than one man can endure

And the drummer plays a mournful sound
The bugler he blows his horn
Forty odd days in the trenches Lord
I just wanna go back home

So I'll write my name on the sleeve of my coat
In blood so someone will see
When they come for the bodies after this war
They'll know that this soldier was me

WHEN DARKNESS COMES
(Recorded on Real 2008)

When darkness comes
What do you do
Do you hide away for hours
Anything to make it through
There in the shadows
With nothing left to lose
When darkness comes

When darkness comes
There's another side
In the thick of it, it's hard to see
But it might turn the tide
There in the shadows
There's a little light
When darkness comes

When darkness comes
And you know it will
You can break the spell with faith
To a place where all is still
There in the shadows
You can drink your fill
When darkness comes

TALK TO ME
(unreleased)

I won't be shackled by the things you've said
Do you really know what's going on
Inside my head
I'm like a book that you've never read
Or cared to

Do we really know what this is all about
I'm hoping maybe this time we can
Figure it out
Cause the last thing I want to do
Is scream and shout
At you

They say the apple doesn't fall far from the tree
There's more than a little bit of you
Inside of me
But that doesn't mean I won't
Turn out differently
All I'm asking is would you
Talk to me

This ain't a contest of who's right
There's nothing left to prove, no need for us to fight
I think we're both blinded by the sight
Of winning

But I ain't gonna love you any less
You'll always be my mother
And I, your little mess
But we'll push each other's buttons
Put this love to the test
Forever

LOOKING FOR GLORY
(Recorded on Real, 2008)

I took a little driving trip across the big wide country
Had a thought that I would travel east
To find a little glory
Took my guitar and some pretty songs
I was looking for adventure
Had had a belly full of working life
Wanted free from my indenture

With every mile I travelled south
I was sure it'd be the last time
I had to venture this far out
To hit the music gold mine
I'd be more than just a local kid
Singing for a story
I'd make my mark, I'd claim my prize
I'd revel in the glory

When I got to Nashville I was sure
I'd be the next discovery
I'd be lauded by the people there
And I wouldn't have to worry
But to my surprise the town was just
Another sea of dreamers
Only difference being I suppose
There were sharks among the swimmers

So I loaded up and headed west
Back to the place I came from
With my tail between my legs I guess
The lure of stardom long gone
I suppose you might say I was sad
And just a little sorry
But there's truth in what I'm saying here
There's a price to pay for glory

RUCKUS IN THE HENHOUSE
(Recorded on A Different Place, 2004)

There's a ruckus in the henhouse
Fox has got control
Finger on the trigger
And a blind eye on the world
With everybody watching
He's dealing in God's name
Just you wait, before you know it
There'll be no one left to blame

Everything is holy
Scripture is for sale
Faith is on the auction block
And God is old and frail
We're bowing to an idol
Spending with our blood
Terror is a currency
And we cannot stop the flood
Everybody's praying
Too loudly to be heard

What we need is a miracle
A way to make it sane
We really must be crazy
If we let things stay the same
What we need is a miracle
A blinding bolt of fire
Burn this cloak of apathy
In the name of liberty

We sit here on the left hand
While the right one's making deals
Watch him on the TV
Trying to tell us how to feel
We're scared but won't admit it
That the bad guys won the war
They're showing dirty pictures
Of what they've been fighting for
Seems like everybody's paying
Too much for what it's worth

ROBINSON CARUSO BLUES
(Recorded on A Different Place, 2004)

I put a message in a bottle
From a little piece of sand
Saying if you get this
Send a signal please
I'm stranded on this island
With nothing but my hands
Floating on an ever changing sea
Feeling just a little seasick
Don't know if I can make it through
If you stop to read this
Understand that I've
Got the Robinson Caruso Blues

Do you ever stop to wonder
Bout the state of your affairs
How easily you forget to dance
Something that's so basic
As the taking in of air
You leave entirely to chance
Slowing down is not an option
There always seems too much to do
You gotta put yourself in my shoes
On this lonely desert isle
With the Robinson Caruso Blues

Well I'm writing this to warn you
My fate is not unique
Our lives are probably the same
When you least expect it
You'll be fighting for your life
And tomorrow becomes the only game
All you care about is sinking
You're caught up in the great expanse of blue
And the next thing that you know
You'll be singing along
To the Robinson Caruso Blues

AUNT KITTY
(Recorded on A Different Place, 2004)

My aunt Kitty was an artist
A headstrong Leo girl
Wrote poetry, wore purple
was the centre of my world
But the day that she turned 60
Started losing track of time
Little things were gone
As the memory that defined her
Slipped away

They all said she was crazy
In her violet and blue
But her spirit kept me focused
It was how I made it through
Now it's really hard to see her
In her powder pink beret
When she can't remember where she is
Or what she did today
It's all slipped away

Sits in her apartment
Trying to hide her fear
Waiting for a lover
Who's been dead 40 years
Silently weeping, tears running down her face
Watching the pieces start to fade

I look at those old photos
Of the way she used to be
Bright eyed no fear
Staring boldly back at me
But I see those eyes are dim now
And she doesn't look the same
I know she feels her hand in mine
But she can't recall my name
It's all slipped away

My aunt Kitty was an artist
A headstrong Leo girl

STARLIGHT PARADE
(Recorded on A Different Place 2004)

I still remember a night such as this
Watching the harbour lights fade
You in my arms, a passionate kiss
One last lover's embrace
With tears in my eyes, I bid you adieu
And this was the promise we made
Whenever you miss me just look overhead
I'll be in the starlight parade

Night after night as I gazed at the stars
I knew that you would be too
I held you close deep in my heart
Feeling connected to you
Though I was fearful you might not return
I thought of the promise we made
It brought me comfort knowing that you
Were up in the starlight parade

I still see the telegram bordered in black
That said you'd been killed at D'amarie
I felt my heart stop with the thought
You'd been taken from me

Years have gone by, there's a grey hair or two
But those memories don't fade
It brings me comfort knowing that you
Wait in the starlight parade
Save the last dance, I'll soon be with you
Up in the starlight parade

GUITAR

You stare at me
from across the room
cracks forming
in your belly

I've neglected you of late
I'm sorry
But life has a way of
creeping inside

It's not your fault
You are only as great
as the hands that caress you
and I've been remiss

But I can make you sing
by rubbing your neck
to ease the tension headache

I can make you cry
by touching you
softly now
harder as we move together

I can make you
whisper
and yet growl
like an animal in heat

But one thing
I cannot do
is forget you

TAKE ME BACK
(unreleased)

Another cheap motel with sheets that smell
Like someone else has been here
Another breakfast place with greasy plates
And the taste of last night's stale beer
Busking for dollars till someone hollers please
No more songs we can't sing to

Back on the two lane, road kill blood stained
Heading for the next town
Sold out gas pumps, too many speed bumps
Slowing me down
Looking for lights in the night up ahead
So at least I can stop moving

More bad coffee, trying to stop the sleep
That keeps coming
This roller coaster, burnt out toaster
Feeling that keeps humming
Can't be courageous when the pages on the map
Start to look like snakes and ladders

Eyes get blurry nature's fury's
Beating on the windshield
Keep the focus, I'll get through this
Clutching the wheel
So many miles all the while thinking that
I'm getting so much closer

Take me back to my old hometown
Put my feet down on some comfortable ground
Stop these wheels from spinning round
Take me back

DREAM AUCTION

They held an auction of my dreams
Each one laid out
in neat little lots
waiting for the bidding to start

Lot 157
the dream of becoming a writer at 19
sold to the woman in the blue sweatshirt
who claimed it for her very own

Lot 180
the dream of having children
sold to the man in the white coat
who so easily collected these
types of dreams every day

Lot 219
the dream of driving a car
sold to the man in the red plaid shirt
He's going to add it to his trophies
he's collected in his 18-wheeler

Lot 417
This is a collection of small dreams
some more important than others
Sold to the consortium

from the bureau of ethical behaviour
They will add it to their
dusty file folders

Lot 521
The dream of peace
sold to the man in the back row
He's squirreling these away
for that proverbial day
when it will make him a lot of money

Lot 1200
Sorry folks
This lot has been withdrawn
Seems the owner wants to keep it
after all

WOMAN

Woman stands
waiting at the well
arms bare
to the sun
feet sore
from standing
she brushes the
sweat from her brow
and sighs

Woman sits
waiting on the porch
eyes closed
to the setting sun
In her breast
the fear
for her children
long gone from
this home
she brushes the flies
from her face
and sighs

Woman lies
awake in the night
listening for the sounds
of feet on the floor

Caught in Time

She tries not to think
of the passing of time
as she brushes the tears
from her eyes
and sighs

Woman holds
arms
too shy to care
cleans the blood
and tears
of the fallen
and gets up again
she sighs

I COULD HAVE SAID

I could have said
let's give it another go
but that would have meant
eating my own words
one more time
and clenching
my already tight lips
one more time

I could have said
Wouldn't it be great
if we just sailed along
not caring if it's good or not
but that would have meant
one more night of
swearing at the dashboard
as I drove home

I could have said
it's only a hobby, a harmless pass time
but that would have meant
giving only 50%
when my body and soul
cried out for 200%

I could have said
I don't want to hurt your feelings
but that would have meant
I'd be hurting mine
and you would never know

Caught in Time

I could have said
it's okay if you don't
really care to step up
I will forgive you
no matter what you do or say
but that would have meant
at some point in my life
I would have had to do
exactly what I just did

So shoulda, coulda, woulda
I did what I did
and all the could have beens
are now resting peacefully....

Caught in Time

TIME

I'm of a mind
that time is behind me
taking a chunk from my rear
It's like I go forward
this hurtling toward
Something I'm sure I will fear

Time has a habit
Oft like a rabbit
leaping about in a hole
before you know it
you're old and you show it
for time has taken its toll

I'm thinking that drinking
might lessen the shrinking
though time may have other plans
like stepping beside me, behind me
to ride me
and wreck havoc on my hands

I used to believe I was young and alive
with nothing but time on my side
now I am sure that I'm feeble and old
Cause my ole buddy time is tired
Or maybe it's time that gets younger each day
sucking the life from me

Caught in Time

the smaller I get the greater he gets
and soon there'll be nothing to see

So ole time my friend
Go back in your cage
Slow down, take a load of your feet
There's no need to hurry, to bustle and worry
And we sure don't need to compete

I'm sure with a little gentle nudge
You can take a vacation or two
Cause lord knows you need it
Go get your feet up
And leave me to live without you

YOU ARE NOT YOUR WORDS

If you have searched for words
In the darkest moment of torment
Or that grief-fuelled state of non-being
You thought by pure virtue
Of your phrases
You had succeeded, you do not understand

You know you can speak
Eloquently and with passion
You can give comfort and solace
But your words spoken are as platitudes

Empty in their sound
Falling on deaf ears
Like white noise
Those who know you
Expect this greatness from you
And turn away when words fail

You live by your words
You hide in their rhythm
You take pride in their ease
Of explaining what you cannot

But there are times
When you are not your words

YOU SPOKE

You spoke to me
with the language of your heart
that stripped bare
wordless language
without the acuity
of the mind

It rang true
as only this can
in a way that made me
weep

I listened
not with my ears
but with my stomach
and lungs
a vibration so simple
it shook me

How could I resist
You didn't need to press
I was yours
body and soul
connected and held

It was truth

NOISE

He banged a drum
With absolute abandon
Arms flailing about
Eyes closed
No thought to the
Outside world

His foot beat
A tattoo rhythm
On the bass drum
While his hands
Tapped the high hat
And snare

He was lost
In this rapture
In this cacophony
Of sound

There was no point
No beat
No song
He was playing
It was the pure
And utter joy
Of noise

OLD MAN

Old man rest now
your time is almost over
you have fought a good fight
but now is not the time for fighting

Old man rest now
your heart is full
know you are welcome
in this ether world
and your time for fighting is over

Old man rest now
send your light to a little one
she needs your spirit
as your body casts away
send it to her
to begin her fighting

Old man rest now
you are welcome here
your spirit can help another
send her your strength
you who have much in abundance
her time for fighting
has just begun

I SEE YOU STANDING

I see you standing
just beyond the edges of the mirror
Old speckled glass
bevelled so the light wavers like water

I see you standing
in the hallway just deep enough
in the shadows to make a darker shadow
dust motes in the air
whisper as you pass

I see you standing
reflected in the light of a passing car
It rolls over you
like water over driftwood
changing the light as it moves

I see you standing
in the bank of an old tree
dark shape outlined by white snow
pointing to the four corners
indistinct but solid

I see you standing
beside the stones bent over to caress them
Old memories call me to look up
and I see you

FROM NOTHING I AROSE

From nothing I arose
Blended skin with the taste of my forefathers
From nothing I arose
Twisted winding hair from my mothers
I carry their spit, their blood and the words
I carry their ideals, their pain and the heart

From nothing I arose
On two feet I carried the wounds of my children
From nothing I arose
I watched the dead fall again and again
I carry their memory, their shine and desire
I carry their joy, their stories and the song

From nothing I arose
A mass of chattering monkey brain
From nothing I arose
Tired of travelling but too addled to sit still
I carry the mantle, the depth and the feeling
I carry the torch, the coal and the stone

I will carry on, it is my fate
I will carry on, it is my gift
I will carry on, for nothing will stop me
      I will carry on, for to nothing I'll return

BLACK FRIDAY

I was 24 that day in '39
They call it Black Friday now
But it was a day like any other day
Ole Frank Burns rang up to say
There was a fire burning
At the pine plantation and
Would I like to come along to see it

I seen a little fire on the telly
Fought with bulldozer, a grader
11 tankers and helicopters
All to fight a scrub fire we could
Have put out with 20 men
I grabbed my horse and my rake
And went along to see

It was a fire all right,
burning in the dry top of the ridge
It went right across the Rubicon
Another 20 miles
I got to working with the other boys

Me with my rake
Them with crosscut saws and shovels
It looked like we'd made a difference
But she'd only pulled in for the night
The wind had other plans
Blowing fearsome, hot from the north west
That fire roared its presence
We couldn't do anything

Caught in Time

We couldn't go anywhere
We bedded down in the bush
In the heat of the day
So we could fight it in the cool of the night
But we weren't making no difference
That fire was burning hungry

We found Ruth just lying in the road
Clutching tobacco and looked to be sleeping
She must have died from the smoke

Hermon's sawmill went up
in the middle of the firestorm
All them trees just disappeared
No stumps, no nothing, like they'd never been there
The river dried up
14 miles up the Acheron Way
They say the river actually stopped running

For three hours
We did our best, we fought it
It came to rest
Sated like with a full belly
It took seventy-one lives that day
And burned to the ground over five million acres

It's a day I won't ever forget
Funny how it was Friday the 13, January 1939

BROWN GIRL

I walked into
this mess
Duppy flying in red mist
tied to calabash bowl
drinking blood from
fresh killed
where he gets them
don't know
stupidness

I walked into
bolem on my hip
tied like apron strings
spit drool milk colour
duds too sore to leak
So to give no name baby
stupidness

I walked into
sweet brown boy
smell like bleach
and spin sugar in my ears
ooo big hands
warm muscle thinking
what was I thinking
no good no count
stupidness

I walked into
old woman
with crazy eyes

one going sideways
one seeing behind me
all yellow and old
smell like old sage
too burnt to be any good
house all torn up
with old age
stupidness

bad man got duppy slave
feed fresh blood
to keep working
red mist
come take my flesh
if I let him
stupidness

no Papa to hear prayers
too many folks talking
Send low ones
Prince of Cemetery
come take bones to cross over
babies him too
to start new life
which he take eventually
stupidness

SLOW

I stand
In the shadow
Of this tree
Bathed
In dappled sunlight
And green

I feel
My heart
Begin to beat
Just a little slower

There is a wisdom
In this old oak
Hundreds of years
Of standing
Silent and aware

Watching
The evolution of man
Two hundred years
To grow a few feet

There is a lesson
I can learn from this
That patience
And time
Accomplish much
Things do not
Happen overnight

It is years and years
Of steady standing
That make the mighty

FULL MOON

Too many women
work here
It's like
feeding time at the zoo
when the full moon appears

Chocolate
tears
and too much drama

And we all feel it
when that ole full moon
comes around

Lord, give me
a group of men
who only pretend
to howl at the moon

FATHER

Father what have I done
I've no recompense for you
I have lived as your son
Wishing nothing more than truth
And even as I sit in death
You won't see this through

Father, I'm not finished
There are things still to be said
It was your name that I cried out
As the blows rained on my head
And I wish for your forgiveness
Even more so now I'm dead

Father, you're not a bad man
It was hard for you to see
But I'm also not a poor lad
I was who I meant to be
There's no justice, that's a given
But you cannot let this be

Father, hear my story
Told through those who know me well
Though it's kind of in the past now
It is their respect as well
Treat them kindly in the meantime
It is something they should tell

I pray with all my heart now
That you'll take a stronger stand
And know the life I chose to lead
Was the merit of this man

MY STORY

My story is like a forest
Called from earth's great bounty
Standing proud for man's reminding

My story is like the night birds
Winging their way without words
Yet speaking volumes of history
And keeping alive the mystery

My story is as old as the mountains
I stood naked in the fountain
And I wore my skin like a mantle
Until the light became a handle

Down down I travel
Splitting, twisting, I unravel
The voices too many to notice
The voices too loud to hold in

My story is rife with music
I dance in my own tunes and two step
A galaxy born in rhyming
A whisper bent on clamouring

Down down I travel
Splitting and twisting I unravel
The tale too long for telling
The magic too little revealing

HAIKU #1

Red leaves on the ground
Rattling in the winter wind
Beautiful in death

SIDES

Side of beef
Beef cake
cake walk
walk about
about nothing
nothing else
else what?
up in the air
air plane
plain crazy
crazy legs
legs diamond
diamond in the rough
rough trade
trade ship
ship of fools
fools gold
gold record
record breaking
breaking glass
glass house
house party
party down
down under
under foot
foot hold
hold off
off side

WE GATHER

We gather
sisters three
to speak
each in our own tongue
robes drawn
around us in warmth

We gather
sisters three
to open our hearts
and tell tales
of longing and love

We gather
sisters three
to take pen to paper
and weave words
from thoughts and feelings
long held

We gather
sisters three
to learn of our pain and peace
to cluck in sympathy
and hum in tune

We gather
sisters three

to throw this to the four corners
and revel in the echoes
coming back to us
a thousand fold

In the stillness of everything
we are sisters
and we smile
across the miles
knowing we are
connected

EVERYTHING I

Everything I ever wanted
was held
in the palm of my hand
a baby bird
so fragile
waiting to fly

Everything I ever feared
was put into my heart
and built a cage
for that bird

SHE'S THE GIRL
(Released on A Different Place 2004)

She's the girl that everybody loves
She's got that something boys dream about
When the show is done and everyone's gone home
She drinks

She's the girl who's everybody's pal
A quick one with the joke, a good time party gal
But when the boys depart, it's then she falls apart
She's the girl that everybody loves

What goods adulation when all she every hears
Is the constant repetition of you're beautiful my dear
Just once she'd like to wake up
And know that she appears to one boy in the world
As a simple hometown girl

She's the one who's everybody's friend
She'll keep their secrets safe, hang on to the bitter end
In a lonely hotel room, she'll toast the fading moon
She's the girl that everybody loves
She's the girl that everybody loves

GYPSY

Dark firelight
flickers
on the edge
of her dream

The musk smell
of sweat
and unwashed
bodies

Rough wood
creaking wheels
herald
the return of
the wagon

brightly painted
with bold colours
and signs
to ward off evil

She sings
in a low voice
made weary by
whiskey
and smoke
of love lost
and love returned

Caught in Time

Notes fly
around the fire
and settle
like ash
on the sleeping

She waits
and closes her eyes
to find
that place
in her heart
where the gypsy
sleeps

ANIMAL'S EYES

We are not alone here
This earth is a crowd of many
We do not manage the wild
It has existed long before
we knew life

We are not masters here
We are the predators and prey
And we fight for survival

We are not victims here
We did not plan for your kind
You came and you
created this world crowding us

We see much more than you seem to
We feel pain
more than you know
We love unconditionally
And cannot comprehend
that you do not see this or us

RHYTHM

Dance me round
the moon
Let me feel the night air
cold on my skin
Warm with your hands
touching mine

Dance me in
the dawn
Let us wash in the morning dew
and feel the burr
of your face
as we kiss

Dance me in the
heat of midday
Sweat and sweat
body heart beating
to cool the fever

Dance me
towards aging
Let me feel the rhythm
as we walk
towards the end

UNDERSTANDING

I asked you for
a little understanding
It wasn't much to ask
Just a little time
to think through what
I felt

I asked you to be
strong
To let down your guard
enough to try and see
what I was going through
just a wee bit of bending

I asked you to feel
my heart
to lean in and listen
to the beating
in my breast
perhaps to hold it
for a moment

I asked you to stop
thinking
to stop the hurt
you think I'd done

Caught in Time

and forgive me
for it
To let down your
guard
and walk awhile with me

I look at you
and see the reflection
of me
staring back with a different face
but so the same
I stare in wonder
knowing that
your understanding can only
come when
I forgive myself

THROUGH THE GARDEN GATE

Through the garden gate I crept
quiet as a mouse
to get to the pathway
that led me to the house

Through brambles, vines and bushes
more than a little overgrown
I wondered at my madness
to touch the ancient throne

Of the king and his wisdom
long forgotten in this place
made green by moss and algae
on his eroded face

A bird is singing overhead
but no joy is in that sound
for the king will not be coming
he's left this hallowed ground

So I wander past the fountain
now filled with leaves and silt
and I place my hands upon the stand
where knights so humbly knelt

I hear again the voices
of the ladies as they cried
When word was passed around the court
that the grand olde king had died

Caught in Time

I do not know what I expect
to find within this place
more than like a graveyard
with its life all but erased

I have fought and I have travailed
but I'm no further on I fear
for the house is there but still afar
and I am no longer near

So I'll leave this path behind me
and close the garden gate
for this graveyard is a sacred place
and the stones will always wait

HONOURING

I remember there's a reason
why today is the day it is
There's no memory of it
in my conscious mind
but it still exists

I've not had to fight for freedom
I've not had to starve or die
There's no law that tells me
What I can't do
No enemy planes fly

I've not seen blood shed on
The city streets I walk
I've not cringed in fear
And heard the dictators evil talk

I don't know poison pens
Nor propaganda's sting
I've not been sent to prison
For every little thing

I don't know how it might feel
To lose loved ones in a war
I've only heard the stories
Of those who've gone before

Caught in Time

If I look into the eyes
Of the veterans here who stand
I am saddened by what I see
But I really don't understand

So on this day of remembering
I hope that I will be
Standing once in silence
And soulful reverie

Trying to remember
And understand what they have seen
And pray it will never come to pass
That the veteran there is me

EXPLOSION

I held my heart
In a box
Protected from the storm
of emotions

It was safe there
Carefully padded
in velvet

I walked around
knowing that no one
could see my heart
but me
when I chose to
take it from the box

Today I felt a stirring
like gases
Bubbling 'neath the surface
of a long dormant
volcano

And I realized
the careful padded
velveteen box
was a cage

FAREWELL

How can I tell you
goodbye
It is with deep regret
and sadness
that I let myself
let go of you

How can I tell you
I'll miss you
Like a part of me
taken
when I still feel you
so deeply

How can I tell you
I know it's time
There are too many words
used to say goodbye
and none of them
are any good

They do not express
what I feel
They cannot convey
what I want to say
They do not understand
the hole that can
never be filled

Goodbye my friend
May we meet again

I FEEL THE CLOCK TICKING

I feel the clock ticking
Down the hours of my life
Every breath I take another second
Towards eternal night
And I wonder in between
Will I ever get this right
I feel the clock tick ticking
Down the hours of my life

I feel the bones aging
Ever slowly but nonetheless
I'm bound in this body
This beautiful mess
And even though I'm mortal
Fire burns within my breast
I feel the bones aging
Ever slowly but nonetheless

I feel my past calling
Every time I tried and failed
I feel the weight of longing
The regrets now old and frail
Though I may have stumbled
I have lived to tell the tales
I feel my past calling
Every time I tried and failed

I feel the soft whisper
As death approaches near
I know that it is coming
I would hope I feel no fear
For this life lived
Is so precious and so dear
I feel the soft whisper
As death approaches near

I feel the clock ticking
Down the hours of my life
But I won't keep on worrying
It won't keep me up at night
I'm a human being
It's everybody's strife
I feel the clock ticking
Down the hours of my life

FLYING

I flew in my dreams
last night
I was weightless
and free
swimming breaststrokes
through the air

I flew in my dreams
last night
sitting on a carpet
made of feathers
and old dog hair
I sang songs
in a strange tongue
and laughed
though I might fall

I flew in my dreams
last night
turning cartwheels
in the clouds
looking at the earth
covered in snow
and whispering
magic spells
and incantations

I flew in my dreams
last night
no worry, no money
I was soaring

Caught in Time

like a silver bird
arms flapping
hell bent for leather
and following the geese

I flew in my dreams
last night
wishing for all the world
that I could leave
this atmosphere
of gravity and ozone
and fly to another
universe
and still be me

GREEN

Envious of the almighty dollar
And its hold on her
She looked the one-eyed monster
In the eye
and prayed she wouldn't give in

Every lucky charm she'd ever held
Felt useless and dull
Like brass left
Too long in the rain

Mould growing on the edges
She lifted it up
And peeked underneath
looking for that first sign
Of renewal

SUNRISE

I walked today
along the treeline
in the blazing morning sunrise
Quiet not even the birds
were stirring

The broken stalks of
last year's feed corn
poking through the snow
Wind whipped drifts
piled left and right
along the roadside

I listened for a minute
to my mind's constant chatter
and found myself
talking out loud
in response
call and answer

I paused
A voice whispered
so low I would have missed it
again, the voice
No words I could understand
just a feeling

I closed my eyes
and inhaled
a respite at the hidden spring

It has called me before
But this glorious morning
In its quiet way it led me here

Old woman in the water
picking seaweed for her daughter

HURRICANE

We sat huddled in the basement
with candles and flashlights
Mom had brought blankets down
from the attic
that smelled of mothballs

We could hear the thunder and lightening
cracking overhead
and the wind whipping at the windows
so hard we'd thought they'd break

Mom lit candles
and started to sing
Old lullabies from when we were kids
It calmed us as we sang along

Dad being Dad, kept checking
the door to the outside
The wind was whistling
He was quiet
and we knew he was worried
but Mom kept singing
and holding us close
in those mothball blankets

We looked out
the sky was green
and crackling with
live wires
the storm was still raging
and the windows were
breathing

Caught in Time

But Mom kept singing
and we knew if we made
it through the night
we'd be okay

We fell asleep
Morning rose
dark and surly
We stepped out
of the basement
to a gentle rain
and grey skies

We made it
through another storm
and we felt blessed

MY BED AS A CHILD

A crib
bars on the window
bright coloured plastic
hanging down
sheets smelling of Ivory soap
a clock ticking

A twin bed
my sister in the bed
next to me
chenille bedspread
and posters of Donny Osmond
above my head

A double bed
my sister still sharing
the room
red wallpaper
and pink painted dressers
purple shag carpet

A foamie on the floor
hard bones against the cold
basement cement
crying to sleep at night
cold

A queen sized bed
wrought iron bed stead
sheets of cotton
and lavender
a man next to me
sleeping back to back
after the fight

FRIENDS
(Released on Real 2008)

With every mistake I surely have made
There's a good friend that stood by my side
They helped me get through, knew just what to do
Had a shoulder when I needed to cry
In good times and bad times, whatever the sting
They all brought me comfort and joy when I sing
So let's raise a glass
To the old friends who've passed
And the new ones we'll make here tonight

Friends are like gold, more precious than gold
They'll help you no matter the cost
And there's no friend more dear than the one standing here
Or the memory of those you have lost
As we get older we think of the past
Hold on to those friendships, make everyone last
So let's raise a glass
To the old friends who've passed
And the new ones we'll make here tonight

Turn to your neighbour and say how d'ya do
Turn to your children and say I love you

So let's raise a glass
To the old friends who've passed
And the new ones we'll make here tonight

MOONLIGHT

We stood naked
you and I
'neath a new moon
white flesh softly
bubbled with the air
passing oh so soft
across our skin

No masks on our faces
just light transforming
our everyday
into the mystical

I touched your hand
and felt you shiver
across the miles
our hearts twinned
and turning
bound by the light
of the moon

I felt your pulse
It awakened something
in me
like an old bond
now fused
by our naked flesh

We were warriors once
you and I
cut down by
the fear of those
who didn't know
what or who
we'd become

Caught in Time

In death we
parted and came
together
In life
we remembered

I carry you
with me always
you who gave me your heart
to hold
I carry you
in dreams
as the warrior you were
and the being
you're becoming

We stand
bathed in this light
and will stand
forever
visible and touched
only by the turning
of the moon

SESTINA

I stand in blood
to receive your blessing
With every breath
I raise high my hands
Open my heart
and close my head

My head, my head
It pounds with blood
My heart, my heart
It awaits your blessing
Let me feel your hands
take away my breath

I catch my breath
You are in my head
I feel your hands
You are in my blood
No blessing, no blessing
My broken heart

My broken heart
and ragged breath
No blessing, no blessing
I have lost my head
Here take my blood
washed clean from your hands

So white your hands

Caught in Time

So cold your heart
I give you my blood
and the very breath I breathe
To warm your head
and await your blessing

I feel your blessing
and the touch of your hands
anoint my head
and open my heart
I breathe
You are in my blood

This blood of your blessing
This breath on your hands
Your heart in my head

HAIKU #2

Late night sleep deprived
Watching the dawn come up
Not wanting to breathe

THE KEY AT KIANA

They say, the old ones
that there was a time
when the water
softly touched
the shore

Trees grew right
to the water's edge
and the stones
grew smooth
With the tide

They say, the old ones
power lived
in this shore
every rock and tree
sang with the wisdom
of the elders

People came from
miles around
to soak in the energy
and leave renewed

They say, the old ones
that the rocks cried
at the raping of the
earth

and in rage changed
the face of the key
forever

the old ones
went to sleep
waiting for the peoples
to come and give
thanks

CAMERON'S SONG

You wear your words
Like a hair shirt
Raw skin and nerve on fire
The twisted sound
Of anguished nouns
When you expound so dire
Gitane smoke
A private joke
The absinthe choke
That fuels you
You sneer at those
Who dare to pose
In bourgeois clothes
To be you

To decompress
You undress
The righteousness of virtue
Take a bow
You've torn it now
You won't allow the wrong view
Left of base
Bearded face
You erase all pretense
But as a sport
While holding court
You transport the sentence

With sweaty zeal
It's so surreal
The converts kneel before you
Your diatribe
their sweet ride

Caught in Time

Genius pride becomes you
You bear the cost
Of meanings lost
You don't emboss the truth
With words confused
Often abused
It's they who lose and not you
With words confused
Often abused
It's they who lose and not you

UNION STATION

She walked through the doors
carrying her battered guitar case
and a small bag
Everything she owned
was in that bag
The guitar, it was never heavy
no matter how many times
she had to carry it.
A chapter and door closed
behind her

She had walked all morning
carrying that bag and case.
She needed to move
to feel the sidewalk
beneath her feet and
know she was not
stationary
She found herself here

The sun was too bright
It hurt her
Glasses kept sliding down her nose
and no free hand
to push them back

It was early
no one about
Like a science fiction movie
about the end of life on earth
She was not afraid
She set down the guitar

Pushed open the old doors
Creaking on their hinges like
an old lady bending to her roses
Cold gleaming marble floors
shining too brightly
for her tired eyes
Slippery shining
like water on a placid lake
It was cold inside
Cold as a morgue she thought

Caught in Time

The death knell
in a cold marble floor

There was a bench.
Cold sticky
cracked red vinyl
with broken springs
and tarnished chrome
She loved it
So sleek and modern and red
Her favourite colour

She sat
Felt the bending
of the springs
as they caught
her weight
And shifted
Funny how the red
reflected itself
in the marble floor
Red and glistening
Like old blood
dried on the tiles

A train whistle blew
and she looked up
Early morning commuters
bound for nine to five shackles
that tied them
to a cubicle
No smiles, no joy
just the sheer cattle call
of money and
working for a living

She lifted her bag to the bench and
laid her head down to rest
holding her guitar case
in her arms
The sounds of the trains
kept her company
and she slept

THE DOOR IS OPEN

I put my life away
In boxes on a shelf
Everything I'd used
To define myself
I said goodbye to friends
And the town that I'd known
Stepped out in the world
And left my comfort zone

When I started on this trip
Didn't know what I would find
With every mile I stripped
Another layer from my mind
Pulling root up after root
Facing down my fear
Following the signs
Until they brought me here

The door is open
It's long overdue
The door is open
Time to walk on through

I'm seeing for the first time
I haven't got it yet
Walking on this high wire
Without a safety net
Every habit I hold on to
Only pulls me down
It's time to say goodbye
To familiar ground

I'm listening to the voices
Spoken in the wind and rain
Holding me so gently
In the eye of this hurricane
It's ok to stumble
it's ok to fall
Learn to be humble
And accept it all....

THE ENVELOPE PLEASE

Pass the envelope please
Oh don't stand there
And be a tease, please grant us some relief
While we wait with bated breath

Pass the envelope please
as we smile for the press
We're not friends you digress
But to lose is certain death

There's a serious contest here
It's magnitude great and you've made us wait
while you act like a buffoon

So pass the envelope please
We want to go home, we want to be alone
This can't be over too soon

WAITING

We sit idly
waiting for the pilot car
to guide us through
the maze of roads
washed away
in the great flood

Whole sections
of highway gone
Taken down with the force
of Mother Nature's hand
praying for the rains to stop

We sit idly
waiting for the all clear
Thick smoke
hangs like morning fog
on the tree tops
Whole sections burning we're told

No rain
for months on end
Careless cigarette toss
fire
praying for the rains to come

We sit idly
waiting for the pilot car
to guide us through
One car at a time
swimming
in the flood

It's the government's fault

Caught in Time

We can't plant our fields
They're diverting the water
to us
praying for the rains to stop

We sit idly
waiting for the forecast
Rivers drying up
Our cattle dying in the field
No water to drink
No market to sell them

Fourteen states
Without water
Too many states
With too much water

We're flooding
And drowning
Praying for the rains to stop
We're drying up
Soon gonna blow away
Like the dust bowl 30's
Praying for the rains to come

LET TIME TAKE CARE OF THE REST
(Recorded on Deep Water 2006)

We've been through a lot
You and me that's for certain
Both of us had
Expectations to fill
Sometimes the doing
Outdoes the pretending
And anything left
Is just tired and still

I hit the road
With my boot heels burning
Leaving you there
With all you could say
Make no mistake
This is not about winning
It's more just the going
And a price that I'll pay

Think of me fondly
Whenever you're thinking
I can't help my wandering
It's what I do best
Remember the good times
Hold them forever
Let time take care of the rest

I guess you can tell
I'm not a great writer
My letters to you
Have been spotty at best
And I gather you know
I'm no longer in Kansas
That ship had set sail
The last time that we met

Caught in Time

Part of the travelling
Is leaving behind things
Didn't say it was easy
Never is kind

A lot has been happening
Since the last time I saw you
I haven't had time
To give you a call
But it's true what they say
About too little hours
With too much to do
Don't do nothing at all

A PRAYER
(unreleased)

I can't grow in a forest
Of tall straight pines
Everyone the perfect tree
I'd rather live as a spruce
Or a clinging vine
Wrapped around an old oak tree

I won't rest on a mountain
Wet with rain
Everything so lush and so green
I'd rather stand in the desert
On a thirsty plain
And let the water come to me

I won't live in a city
Surrounded by
All those people, noise and things
I'd rather sit in the forest
Of tall straight pines
And let them hear me sing

About the Author

From my earliest memories, I was writing. Songs, little plays, poems, didn't matter. I've always loved words. I started writing songs when I was in my late teens and stopped in my early 20's because friends told me I wasn't any good.

For the next 26 years, I did nothing, no writing, no singing – the Novocain of my own choosing. In my late 40's, I wrote a song on a dare and haven't stopped since – over ten years ago. I've released 4 CDs, written numerous poems and blogs, started a book and plan to write another in the near future.

Writing has been a consolation, a challenge and a curse. But it is what fuels me and keeps me moving forward.

- **Jane Eamon**

Caught in Time

Manor House Publishing

www.ingramcontent.com/pod-product-compliance
Lightning Source LLC
Chambersburg PA
CBHW021119080526
44587CB00010B/573